THE MEANING OF LIFE

BRETT THOMAS

BALBOA.PRESS
A DIVISION OF HAY HOUSE

Balboa Press books may be ordered through booksellers or by contacting:

Balboa Press
A Division of Hay House
1663 Liberty Drive
Bloomington, IN 47403
www.balboapress.com
844-682-1282

Because of the dynamic nature of the Internet, any web addresses or links contained in this book may have changed since publication and may no longer be valid. The views expressed in this work are solely those of the author and do not necessarily reflect the views of the publisher, and the publisher hereby disclaims any responsibility for them.

The author of this book does not dispense medical advice or prescribe the use of any technique as a form of treatment for physical, emotional, or medical problems without the advice of a physician, either directly or indirectly. The intent of the author is only to offer information of a general nature to help you in your quest for emotional and spiritual well-being. In the event you use any of the information in this book for yourself, which is your constitutional right, the author and the publisher assume no responsibility for your actions.

Any people depicted in stock imagery provided by Getty Images are models, and such images are being used for illustrative purposes only.
Certain stock imagery © Getty Images.

Print information available on the last page.

ISBN: 979-8-7652-2806-7 (sc)
ISBN: 979-8-7652-2807-4 (e)

Balboa Press rev. date: 06/02/2022

Dedicated to:

The curious seekers; the plagued, the peaceful, and the all-day-dreamers.

Mid Life Crisis'ers, new lifers, and end of journey decipherers.

To the thinkers, of the "over" variety.

The conformists and the "strange" folks, here, there, and anywhere…

Author's Note

The leading and hopeful idea for "The Meaning of Life" was that fellow human beings would embrace the inherent humor in these pages. A secondary goal was that we might feel the undercurrent of an opportunity for self-exploration and creative expression. Sooo, if by peeking at the following pages you laughed, even a little bit, or broke out a pen (of your choosing), that would be a mission completed!

If I am being honest, I also "wrote" this for the ol' bucket list...anddd to send a little friendly hat tip to the universe, on the backend, or perhaps at the onset, of a wild existential awakening. Many thanks to Ms. Cosmos for the nudge ☺

It is worth mentioning that during the time period when this was created, the entire world was forced to stop and turn inward in so many ways – in early 2020, the Covid 19 global pandemic had changed the landscape of life as we knew it. Amongst the tragedies, strangeness, and conversations that the pandemic produced, *Meaning* never felt more up for grabs.

Before too many run-on sentences break out of the starters' box and take off forever: Thank You for having the curiosity to open this book and the nerve to keep turning these pages...

For those who are challenged to the point of agitation,
Regarding the nothingness of this book's declaration,
I beg you - read it again - to alter the situation,
You may crack a smile or be upset with deprivation.

At home on your coffee table this book may sit,
A conversation piece for guests to talk a bit.
A lighthearted exercise in creation and wit,
Or the idea scares you to the point that you shit.

You might quickly agree with the literal pages,
Or stay a while to experience difference stages,
Perhaps this was a terrible investment for the ages,
But if the front cover caught your attention, then curiosity rages…

It could excite you to where you are singing a song,
Or end up in the trashcan where it probably does belong.
Is there inherent meaning Here or a universal gong?
Do you believe in an answer, right or wrong?

Are we completely separate or One with the Whole?
Do we have free will or is there *really* no control?
In any case, one confession - I do have a goal:
You clutching *the contents of Your book* tightly to your Soul

Will the next page illuminate you, Or lead you to strife?
Either way I hope you enjoy *It*…the "book" and your *Life*.

-BKT

THE MEANING OF LIFE

THE MEANING OF LIFE

THE MEANING OF LIFE

THE MEANING OF LIFE

THE MEANING OF LIFE

THE MEANING OF LIFE

THE MEANING OF LIFE

THE MEANING OF LIFE

THE MEANING OF LIFE

THE MEANING OF LIFE

THE MEANING OF LIFE

THE MEANING OF LIFE

THE MEANING OF LIFE

THE MEANING OF LIFE

THE MEANING OF LIFE

THE MEANING OF LIFE

THE MEANING OF LIFE

THE MEANING OF LIFE

THE MEANING OF LIFE

THE MEANING OF LIFE

THE MEANING OF LIFE

THE MEANING OF LIFE

THE MEANING OF LIFE

THE MEANING OF LIFE

THE MEANING OF LIFE

THE MEANING OF LIFE

THE MEANING OF LIFE

THE MEANING OF LIFE

THE MEANING OF LIFE

THE MEANING OF LIFE

THE MEANING OF LIFE

THE MEANING OF LIFE

THE MEANING OF LIFE

THE MEANING OF LIFE

THE MEANING OF LIFE

THE MEANING OF LIFE

THE MEANING OF LIFE

THE MEANING OF LIFE

THE MEANING OF LIFE

THE MEANING OF LIFE

THE MEANING OF LIFE

THE MEANING OF LIFE

THE MEANING OF LIFE

THE MEANING OF LIFE

THE MEANING OF LIFE

THE MEANING OF LIFE

THE MEANING OF LIFE

THE MEANING OF LIFE

THE MEANING OF LIFE

THE MEANING OF LIFE

THE MEANING OF LIFE

THE MEANING OF LIFE

THE MEANING OF LIFE

THE MEANING OF LIFE

THE MEANING OF LIFE

THE MEANING OF LIFE

THE MEANING OF LIFE

THE MEANING OF LIFE

THE MEANING OF LIFE

THE MEANING OF LIFE

THE MEANING OF LIFE

THE MEANING OF LIFE

THE MEANING OF LIFE

THE MEANING OF LIFE

THE MEANING OF LIFE

THE MEANING OF LIFE

THE MEANING OF LIFE

THE MEANING OF LIFE

THE MEANING OF LIFE

THE MEANING OF LIFE

THE MEANING OF LIFE

THE MEANING OF LIFE

THE MEANING OF LIFE

THE MEANING OF LIFE

THE MEANING OF LIFE

THE MEANING OF LIFE

THE MEANING OF LIFE

THE MEANING OF LIFE

THE MEANING OF LIFE

THE MEANING OF LIFE

THE MEANING OF LIFE

THE MEANING OF LIFE

THE MEANING OF LIFE

THE MEANING OF LIFE

THE MEANING OF LIFE

THE MEANING OF LIFE

THE MEANING OF LIFE

THE MEANING OF LIFE

THE MEANING OF LIFE

THE MEANING OF LIFE

THE MEANING OF LIFE

THE MEANING OF LIFE

THE MEANING OF LIFE

THE MEANING OF LIFE

THE MEANING OF LIFE

THE MEANING OF LIFE

THE MEANING OF LIFE

THE MEANING OF LIFE

THE MEANING OF LIFE

THE MEANING OF LIFE

THE MEANING OF LIFE

THE MEANING OF LIFE

THE MEANING OF LIFE

THE MEANING OF LIFE

THE MEANING OF LIFE

THE MEANING OF LIFE

THE MEANING OF LIFE

THE MEANING OF LIFE

THE MEANING OF LIFE

THE MEANING OF LIFE

THE MEANING OF LIFE

THE MEANING OF LIFE

THE MEANING OF LIFE

THE MEANING OF LIFE

THE MEANING OF LIFE

THE MEANING OF LIFE

THE MEANING OF LIFE

THE MEANING OF LIFE

THE MEANING OF LIFE

THE MEANING OF LIFE

THE MEANING OF LIFE

THE MEANING OF LIFE

THE MEANING OF LIFE

THE MEANING OF LIFE

THE MEANING OF LIFE

THE MEANING OF LIFE

THE MEANING OF LIFE

THE MEANING OF LIFE

THE MEANING OF LIFE

THE MEANING OF LIFE

THE MEANING OF LIFE

THE MEANING OF LIFE

THE MEANING OF LIFE

THE MEANING OF LIFE

THE MEANING OF LIFE

THE MEANING OF LIFE

THE MEANING OF LIFE

THE MEANING OF LIFE

THE MEANING OF LIFE

THE MEANING OF LIFE

THE MEANING OF LIFE

THE MEANING OF LIFE

THE MEANING OF LIFE

THE MEANING OF LIFE

THE MEANING OF LIFE

THE MEANING OF LIFE

THE MEANING OF LIFE

THE MEANING OF LIFE

THE MEANING OF LIFE

THE MEANING OF LIFE

THE MEANING OF LIFE

THE MEANING OF LIFE

THE MEANING OF LIFE

THE MEANING OF LIFE

THE MEANING OF LIFE

THE MEANING OF LIFE

THE MEANING OF LIFE

THE MEANING OF LIFE

THE MEANING OF LIFE

THE MEANING OF LIFE

THE MEANING OF LIFE

THE MEANING OF LIFE

THE MEANING OF LIFE

THE MEANING OF LIFE

THE MEANING OF LIFE

THE MEANING OF LIFE

THE MEANING OF LIFE

THE MEANING OF LIFE

THE MEANING OF LIFE

THE MEANING OF LIFE

THE MEANING OF LIFE

About the Author

Brett Thomas is a believer in people, recovering catholic, retired partier, borderline agonistic, shitty poet, aspiring buddha, hopeful humanist, joke maker and renewed mystic. He was compelled to publish this book as a result of asking himself (and the sky) the same big question; Why? He enjoys long walks down philosophical rabbit holes, particularly whilst in good company. (If you have ever been subject to one of these rabbit holes, please accept his apologies)

Normally, one might tell you that Brett is a creative person with good intentions at heart, but that feels like a lie right now, because you are probably realizing that buying this book was akin to getting a henna face tattoo on a long walk home from a failed bar crawl; only regret and disgust could emerge. Be that as it may, we could forgive him…for now.

He graduated from Villanova University, which not only has nothing to do with this book, but also, the University would probably deny any involvement in this material. To which he may reply: Why was there no course on existential crisises and how to handle them? At this point, you may be aware that Brett himself is writing his own "About the Author" because, well, no one else cared to do it. And with that, he leaves you with a *Virtual Hug* and one big Cheers!

If after reading this masterpiece you decide to explore a little more and perhaps share your unique thoughts on the matter, please feel free to do so at: **www.TheMeaningOfLifeBook.org**

More of Nothing @ **www.TheMeaningOfLifeBook.org**

Printed in the United States
by Baker & Taylor Publisher Services